There's a Bully in my School

by Linda Teed

Illustrated by Monica Paterson

To all the Annabelle Glinton's I've been privileged to know and love. And to my hero with the walker... you know who you are.
I love you.
Philippians 4:13

© 2022 Linda Teed
All rights reserved. No part of this book may be reproduced in any form without permission from the author, with the exception of short quotations for reviews.

Published by Goose Water Press LLC.
www.kristenemilybehl.com

eBook: 978-1-954809-20-8
Paperback: 978-1-954809-15-4
Hardback: 978-1-954809-16-1

Cover design and illustrations by Monica Paterson.

So I did what my mom always told me to do. "Treat others the way you would want them to treat you, Annabelle." I turned around and gave that bully the biggest, sweetest Annabelle Glinton smile I knew how to give. But he just stared at me.

And...I think he growled!

When I went to the lunchroom to eat my favorite bologna and jelly sandwich, the bully was sitting all alone. I heard my mom's words again: "Annabelle, treat others kindly. Kindness will be reciprocated."

So, I strolled up to the bully with my shiny Annabelle Glinton shoes, and with my biggest, best, new-friend voice I asked, "Is someone sitting here?"
But the bully only stared at me and scrunched up his face like an overripe grapefruit.

That made me kind of scared!

Later, when I was writing about Super Jaxy, my flying super-hero basset hound, my pencil broke with a SNAP. I thought I heard the bully snicker! When I stood up to sharpen my pencil, he stuck his foot out and stepped on my shiny Annabelle Glinton shoes!

This time his face looked like he had swallowed a worm. I almost got mad, but then I remembered that my mom said, "Accidents happen."

To top it all off, Mrs. Rodell said the bully would be our Classroom Engine today, even though it was MY turn. Classroom Engine is my favorite job of all time. My shiny Annabelle Glinton shoes didn't feel quite so shiny as I turned to take my place behind the bully, but I smiled at him anyway. Maybe he needs this special job more than I do today, I thought.

Then, when Mrs. Rodell wasn't looking, the bully grinned at me and gave me a tiny shove.

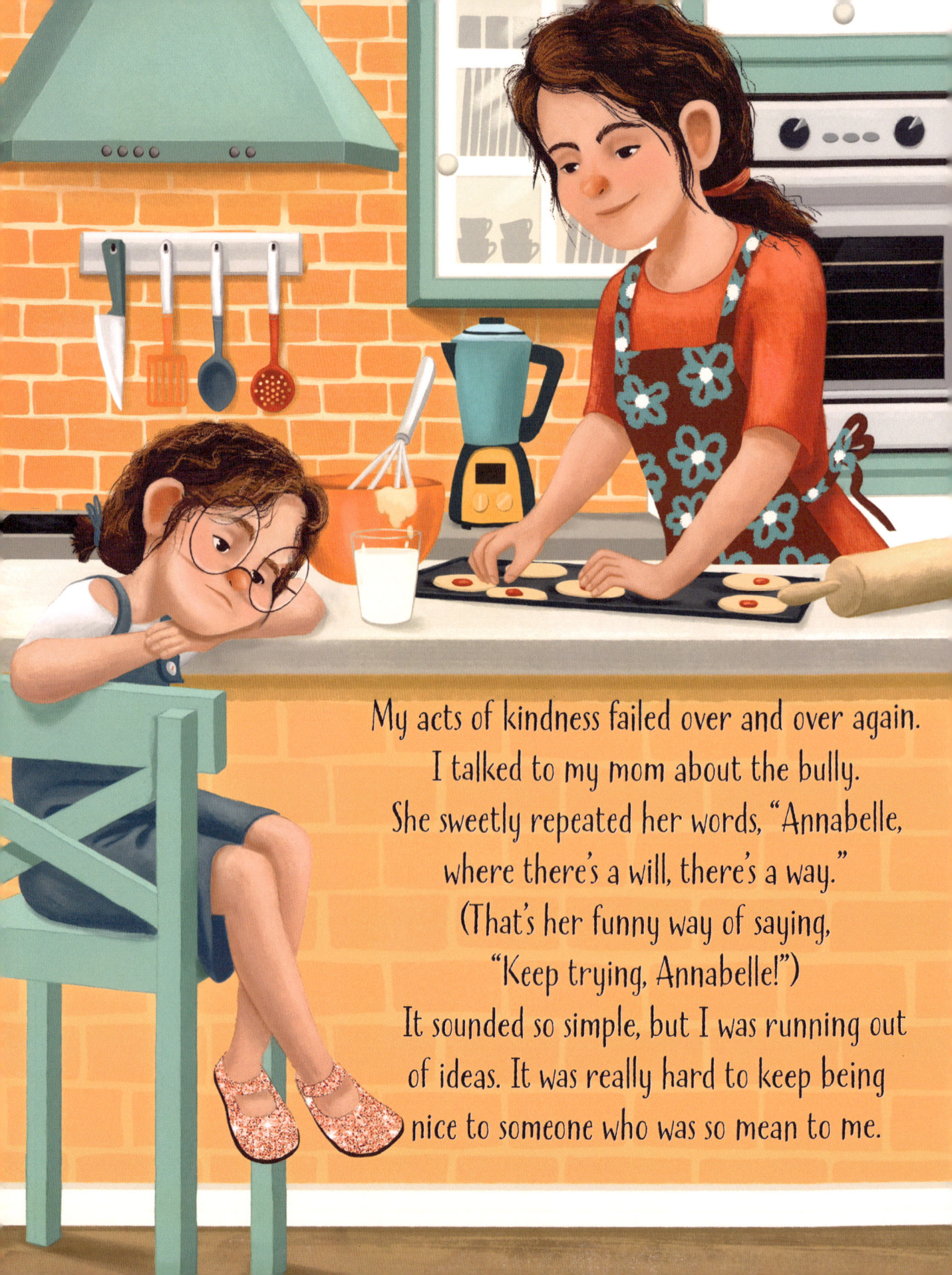

My acts of kindness failed over and over again. I talked to my mom about the bully. She sweetly repeated her words, "Annabelle, where there's a will, there's a way." (That's her funny way of saying, "Keep trying, Annabelle!") It sounded so simple, but I was running out of ideas. It was really hard to keep being nice to someone who was so mean to me.

I even got up the courage to talk to our principal, Mrs. Rodriguez. I told her I thought the bully would never change, and that we should probably ask him to leave because school wasn't so fun since he came around. But Mrs. Rodriguez seemed to side with the bully! She said, "I think he could be a wonderful friend. And who better to show him how to do that than you, Annabelle?"

Talking with Mrs. Rodriguez didn't help me AT ALL!

When I thought things couldn't get worse, when I'd exhausted all my kindest Annabelle Glinton smiles and sweet words, the bully did the meanest thing ever.

He started telling all my friends that my shoes looked silly, and they started to laugh. Then he convinced them that I couldn't possibly kick a ball with my shiny Annabelle Glinton shoes, and I started to be picked last for the soccer games at recess.

And before I knew it, I realized the bully had stolen my best friends.

When the bully had a fancy, shmancy birthday party, he invited all of my friends, but not me.

He didn't even invite his own grandmother!

I tried to win back my friends by making glittery bags with my new sparkly pens. I wrote my friends' names on them in my best cursive writing and filled them with some of my favorite things.

But when I gave them out at recess the next day, my friends all laughed and told me how silly they were. Even my glittery shoes couldn't fix my broken heart.

That night I cried rare Annabelle Glinton tears. I looked out at my favorite star—the brightest, glowiest star in the sky—and I asked God, "Why has all of my kindness turned into something wrong, not something right?"

The next morning I told my mom over pancakes that I needed to start over. "I need to go to a new school so I can find new friends who won't laugh at me." Mom just gave me her warm, love-you smile and said, "Annabelle, running away never solves problems. There will always be people who aren't nice to you. You can't control them. The only person you can control is you."

I wondered and thought and sat quietly while my sparkly Annabelle Glinton shoes continued to gleam.

The next day felt like a whole new beginning; kind of like a new school year feels. The sun was shining and my Annabelle Glinton shoes couldn't have looked any more sparkly! My mom's words, "The only person you can control is you," buzzed in my head.

As I arrived at the playground, I looked right past my old friends and that mean old bully, and I spotted her: the girl with the sad face who always seemed to be sitting alone. The choice became remarkably clear.

With my brightest, glowiest Annabelle Glinton smile I approached her and said, "Hello! My name is Annabelle. My mom just bought me a new glittery jump rope with sparkles and beads inside. Do you want to play with me?"

Her face lit up like the biggest Fourth of July celebration ever!

As we began playing, I wondered why it had taken me so long to understand that true friends are kind. True friends treat each other with love and respect. True friends aren't mean. They aren't bullies.

Do you think I did the right thing?
What would your choice be?

Questions to Ponder:

Why do you think the bully was a bully?
What might have made him that way?

Why do you think the bully's target for his meanness was Annabelle? Was there something about her that made him so mean to her?

Do you think the grown-ups in the story helped Annabelle? Why or why not?

There is a reference to the bully's grandmother in the story. What significance does his grandma play in the story?

The bully is never named. Why do you think this is so?

Explain the things you know about Annabelle. What is missing in her life?

Describe what you think a perfect friend might be. Is there such a thing as a perfect friend?

Why do you think Annabelle always wore sparkly shoes? How do they play a part in the story?

The friend Annabelle meets has no name. Can you name her? Why did you choose the name you did?

Has anyone ever been mean to you?
Have you ever treated someone else unkindly?
How did that make you feel?

Vocabulary Word of the day
inimitable

Linda Teed lives in a humble little township in the beautiful USA, where she and her husband Patrick raised up three extraordinary kids and earned the new title of grandparents.

When she is not teaching and creating, you'll find her at the library surrounded by all her friends. She dares to "sing about wishes and hearts' desires" and marvels at "the stars' bright twinkling light – a light that destroys the darkness."

Monica currently lives in the UK but she is native to South Africa. Together with her loving (and loved) husband of twenty years, they have raised three wonderful, talented and unique boys - they make her proud to be their mom every day.

As an artist and Graphic Designer, illustrating children's books was the dream job she never even knew she wanted to do. She is so thankful for the ways in which the Lord has led her to this wonderful career and working with amazing authors.

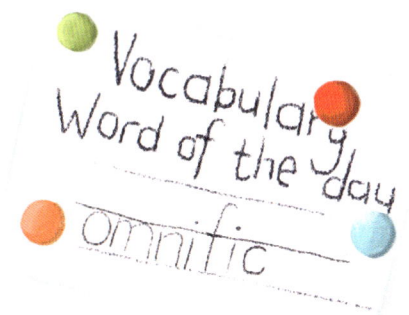

Don't miss these titles from Goose Water Press!

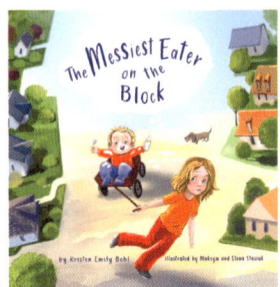

The Messiest Eater on the Block

A frustrated older sister tells her perspective of a little brother with such poor table manners that unwanted dinner guests begin showing up at the door. Get ready to make silly sounds and use your imagination as the young messy eaters in your family learn that they are loved despite—or because of—the messes.

Upendi, a Tale of Hope in Africa

Sadiki enjoys working as a safari guide in the Serengeti. He loves the animals that live there— especially Upendi, the beautiful elephant who reminds him of home. When the visitors suddenly stop coming, Sadiki must go back to his village and find new ways to provide for his wife and children. But soon he realizes that his efforts to feed his family have put Upendi in danger. Will he choose to protect her even when it seems impossible?

The Nest of Chockablock Hair

One special girl, one sweet baby albatross, two lives forever changed.

Meet Maria and Louie--two irresistible friends that meet quite by accident. When they discover a surprising connection, can they work together to find Louie's family? Will Louie give Maria the confidence she needs to make new friends? Be part of the adventure in this series about love, friendship, and the true meaning of home.

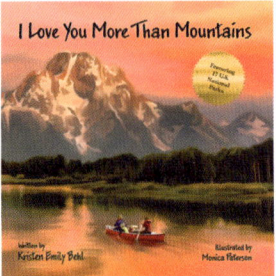

I love You More Than Mountains

Immerse your children in the beauty and wonder of the U.S. National Parks. Help them comprehend how BIG and WIDE, how TALL and DEEP your love for them will always be. These are memories they will never forget!

I'm Too Big to Be This Little

Allie Grace is a little girl caught in a dilemma that every child faces: being too little for some things, yet too big for others. Throughout this humorous and endearing story, Allie Grace learns that there are many things for which she is just the right size!

Printed in Great Britain
by Amazon